The
NORTH

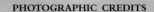

PHOTOGRAPHIC CREDITS

All photographs by CHRISTOPHER HILL with the exception of the
following photographs by Jill Jennings and Robert Malone, members of
the Christopher Hill Photographic staff:

JILL JENNINGS: p.45; p.88 (top); p.94; p.96; p.97; p.98 (top and bottom);
p.99 (top and bottom); p.101 (top).

ROBERT MALONE: pp.90–1 (bottom); p.107 (bottom).

First published in 1995 by
The Blackstaff Press Limited
3 Galway Park, Dundonald, Belfast BT16 0AN, Northern Ireland

© Photographs, Christopher Hill Photographic, 1995
© Text, Ian Hill, 1995
All rights reserved

Typeset by Tony Moreau
Colour Reproduction by DOTS
Printed in Ireland by ColourBooks Limited

A CIP catalogue record for this book
is available from the British Library

ISBN 0-85640-546-9

This page: Silent Valley, Mourne Mountains, County Down
Previous page: Lower Lough Erne, County Fermanagh

The
NORTH
from Down to Donegal

PHOTOGRAPHS BY
Christopher Hill

TEXT BY
Ian Hill

THE
BLACKSTAFF
PRESS

Carrickfergus Castle, even when it's gilded by the evening's sun, sits incongruously apart from the town of its camp followers. But, once-upon-a-time, each Sunday, the castle's bored and sweaty soldiery, plus their pomaded officers bright as peacocks, would have squashed into the pews of the contemporaneous nearby parish church of St Nicholas. There they would have sung lustily, squinnying along the pews for matronly bosums, maidenly waists.

Carrickfergus Castle

But churchgoing Sundays were few in the five centuries after John de Courcy, the colonising Anglo-Norman, built these stout defences on the rock of Fergus. History was a poor comrade-in-arms. In the many wars there were few comforts for the besieged and the castle fell first to King John – he whom the French call Jean sans Terre – subduing de Courcy's protégé, de Lacy. A century later, Bruce, a Scot, harried the English to submission in a twelvemonth.

In 1760 the castle's *farouche* defenders used their pantaloon buttons as shot before surrendering to the French capitaine François Thurot. Offshore, two years later, Scots-born John Paul Jones, founder of the US navy, aboard the *Ranger* forced the battleship *Drake* to strike flag. But in Ulster's iconography these dates are nought compared to the 1690s, when Schomberg took the castle for William III. A plaque marks where King Billy landed.

The drowned Fergus had been Scotland's first king, de Lacy was de Courcy's victor. Niall Mór O'Neill who razed the castle nearly seventy years after Bruce's expedition was a Celt and William Orr, imprisoned there in 1796, was a United Irishman and a Presbyterian. Thus, 'mongst the wards, keeps and dungeons, is the warp, woof and weft of the North's history. Weave in, too, the port's eponymous song of exile, with its slow cadence of the waning tide, and add the words from the poet Louis MacNeice's childhood memories of 'saddened black dreams'.

Now flocks of redshanks pick at the lough's mudflats, but north, at the ferry port of Larne, only three-storey Olderfleet Castle remains of the three castles the sixteenth-century English garrisoned there to keep clear the sea of their despised 'redshanks', the island and highland Scots. Across the narrow mouth of Larne Lough, both 'redshank' and garrison would have seen the capstone of the four-thousand-year-old dolmen now standing in the cottage garden of 91 Ballylumford Road.

Further north, waterfalls tumble – *ess na larach*, the mare's fall, and *ess na crub*, the fall of hooves – from a plateau rich in mound, rath, castle, tomb and dolmen; most genuine, some slightly foxy in their provenance. One such, at Lubitavish, was chosen for local pride to be the grave of Ossian, the poet-warrior son of Ulster's hero Finn Mac Cool. An eighteenth-century antiquary obligingly faked, then discovered and translated, his poems, upon which the province's flintiest twentieth-century poet, the late John Hewitt, left us with an option.

Glenariff waterfall

Hewitt on Ossian:

The legend has it, Ossian lies
beneath this landmark on the hill,
asleep till Fionn and Oscar rise
to summon his old bardic skill
in hosting their last enterprise.

This, stricter scholarship denies,
declares this megalithic form
millennia older than his time –
if such lived ever, out of rime –

. . . let cither story stand for true,
as heart or head shall rule . . .

Eight thousand years ago, Ireland took its leave of the rest of this archipelago and, thus, many birds and plants and fishes never reached its shores. Of those which had arrived before the great divide, some adapted particularly to their new environment. Amongst the sheltering stands of sycamore, deep in Antrim's glens the chirping Irish coal tit has more sulphur-yellow to its chest than its mainland kin. Dipping, diving into the hard head-aching cold of the waterfalls, Ireland's dipper has a particularly distinguishing gorget below every dipper's white chest.

Flighting twixt the conifer stands, the aptly named *scréachóg*, the argumentative moustachioed Irish jay, lacks the white beard of its British cousins and, deep in the wind-cropped heather of the plateau above, the rare Irish red grouse, but a pale shadow of its ruddier relatives east, repeats its unheeded call *go-bak, go-bak* to hunter and traveller alike.

Left: Bluebells, Portglenone, County Antrim
Opposite: Glenariff

On a bluff above Red Bay, more of the stuff of politics. A literary summer school celebrates Hewitt's radical and egalitarian independence, in Garron Tower, a house suitably austere in its black basalt, but ironic in its Rheinsteinian conflations designed to the glory of a nineteenth-century marchioness. Nearby Georgian Drumnasole – built to drawings by Charles Lanyon who gave the North his best – was the house of Francis Turnley.

Turnley was a power in the East India Company, which managed India for the British, or for whom the British policed India. His successor was murdered in the avenue, espousing the cause of his cousin Casement. Roofs and chimneys of Lanyon's many hidden mansions decorate the hinterland, hinted at in whimsical gate lodges. But Clough Williams Ellis's is the square at Cushendun where the English poet Masefield went a-courtin'.

Above: Red Bay
Opposite: Cushendun

Up off the very coast road that Lanyon himself designed, snaking north, linking glen to glen, stooks of corn and hay ricks still dry in isolated August fields. Higher up, on the plateau, once there were ricks of turf drying too. Now almost the only turf rick is in the shape of a windswept peak: Croaghan, the little rick, not big enough to merit a mountain's title of slieve. A raven caws. Far to the east, Scotland's the land across the sea.

Saint Patrick himself they say herded swine, as any saint worthy of posterity was wont to do under duress, on the slopes of Slemish, south. Before him, long long before, hardy-knuckled folk chipped flint tools by the banks of the Glendun, speared salmon and tickled brown and speckled trout. Now hardy-knuckles is but a memory of a schoolboy's game and trout licences are sourced at the village store.

Below: Glendun River
Opposite: Croaghan

The Vikings made their first Irish
landfall here, on Rathlin, and must
surely have felt at home, raiding the
puffin nests for eggs, netting
guillemots for marinading as they
abseiled down the Slievecarn cliffs
120 metres above the cold crashing
wave.

Before that, the Greek geographer
Ptolemy knew enough of it to chart
it as Rikini, and long long before
that? Well there was a stone-axe
enterprise run from the bluestone
outcrop at Brockley. Yes, and
Robert I, known as The Bruce,
contender for the Scottish throne
and on the run from the English
after his ignominious defeat at
Methven, holed up here in a rude
castle on the north-east headland,
taking inspiration in the winter of
1305 – as every schoolchild used to
know – from the perseverance of a
spider, attempting again and again
and at last succeeding to be-web the
seeping walls of a nearby cave.

His resolve thus stiffened, he
returned to his royal quest and took
the throne at Bannockburn. And in
1575 Sir Francis Drake's guns
pounded de Courcy's island castle in
the Elizabethan Wars.
Off shore the swirling Sea of Moyle
was prison to the Children of Lir,
for an eternity turned to swans by
their wicked stepmother.

Rathlin Island

Below: Rathlin Island, view from
Slievecarn towards Fair Head
Opposite (top): Rathlin coastline

In late August, passengers on the last mail
boat out of Ballycastle, heading into the
setting sun, kiss to the tune of the 'Ould
Lammas Fair', hearing in their heads, above
the throb of the ferry's engine and the gulls'
cry, just one half-remembered cadence from
the song's lyric:

But the scene that haunts my memory
Is kissin' Mary Ann,
Her poutin' lips all sticky,
From eatin' Yellow Man.

But such is the stuff of storybook and
tourist's reverie. The reality of Rathlin's
history is as bloodied as any. Viking pillage
meant two hundred years of rape, torture,
slavery and death. In 1597 the English Lord
Essex put the MacDonnell women and
children to the sword, axe and bludgeon
whilst their men watched from the mainland.
Every last one of the descendants of those
who survived fell to Archibald, Earl of
Argyll, forty-five years later. Look up from
the hollow of Lag-a-vriste-vor even on a
bright windswept day and sense the day the
place took its meaning 'the hollow of the
great defeat'. Above is Crook Ascreidlin, 'the
hill of the screaming', from where their
women watched.

Below: Carrick-a-Rede rope bridge
Right: Aerial view of Carrick-a-Rede
Opposite: Carrick-a-Rede, looking
towards Larrybane

If the female Irish salmon survives the nets, great boxes of mesh as big as houses placed by the fishermen off Carrick-a-Rede, she turns up river into the Bush to dig a concave redd for her eggs in up-river gravel, over which her mate will ejaculate his milt. The alevin emerge three months later and those that survive the voracious river creatures turn to fry and then to parr. In a year, finger length, as black-and-red-spotted parr, they turn to sea again, becoming the elegant silver smolt as they do. A year and two thousand nautical miles pass before some will come back as grilse to run the nets, refuse the fly. Or maybe it will be in two years or three, blue and silver, to spawn. And perish. Or to limp down river, a wasted, unwanted, kelt.

Below: Whitepark Bay
Right: The Ladies', at
Whitepark Bay

The air round Carrick-a-Rede is sliced with the call of black guillemot, razorbill and kittiwake, the last species obligingly calling its own name. Stand high on the rock and the fulmar sweep beneath, delineating the cliff edge's billowing updrafts.

Beyond Carrick-a-Rede is Sheep Island, once called Puffin Island when puffins were plentiful. Puffins are few now and the rocks are white with the guano of the massed poised cormorants.

In Whitepark Bay chequerboard oystercatchers nip and tuck at the rush and fall of each wave. Plover and sanderling peck mechanically where wet and dry sand meld. Skylark spiral into the glorious summer blue; linnets flick from shrub to winter shrub. A stonechat's call pierces the rhythm of each wave's tumble and retreat.

Eider duck bob beyond the surf. The flutter-by of the common blue butterfly strikes a lambent chord with the harebell's trembling petal. Cows chew, deposit pats. Human lovers, impatient, lust once again for no other love. And above, the buzzard scans for the plump rock dove.

The tossed, tumbled and plundered stones of
Dunineny Castle, quit just before his death, in
1590, by the ninety-year-old, still flaxen-haired
Sorley Boy MacDonnell, are scattered across the
cliff top, west of Ballycastle. Colla, his black-haired
brother, lived sullenly in his shadow. But now the
ruins of Colla's black basalt castle, perched
chiaroscuro on a chalk-white, almost-island rock at
Kenbane, are the more impressive. A stream rushes
from the cliff above, waves roll the rounded beach
stones in the crescent of its bay. It would have
been a hardy sword which faced its challenge. For
this is a coast not just of crescent bays and quaint
ports. It is a coast of castles, nightmares, histories
and stories. And for almost every story there is a
MacDonnell, and for the ones which have no
MacDonnell in them, there's a more ancient tale of
sad goddesses, rough giants and star-crossed lovers.

There's Dunseverick Castle, its sixteenth-century
gatehouse but a poor thing now. Deirdre of the
Sorrows died, at her own hand, on the unfriendly
shore where the scant ruins now pose. Betrothed
to Conor, merciless as kings are in legends kept to
support the rule of law, she glimpsed his
bodyguard Naoise across the flickering rush lights
of the fort of the Red Branch Knights at Emain
Macha and was lost to crown for ever.   Whitepark Bay

The lovers fled to Scotland across the Sea of
Moyle, with Naoise's two brothers riding point.
Fergus, an ambivalent, cunning and ambitious
politician at Conor's court, himself a man with
an eye for the lady (and who at the subsequent
Commission for Truth and Justice claimed
himself an improbably naïve and innocent foil)
pleaded their return and vouchsafed the king's
pardon.

But when they landed at Dunseverick by
Bengore Head to travel south to Conor's base at
Emain Macha, the king's mercenaries put all the
brothers to the sword and the king himself
despoiled Deirdre, who hurled herself onto the
rocks and died. Crazed Fergus, his plans asunder,
razed all about.

Another legend says that Conall, who witnessed
the Crucifixion and the laying of Jesus in his
tomb, had his home here too and once it was
amongst the three great buildings of Ireland, the
capital of the kingdom of Dál Riata to which all
roads led, and cited such by every storyteller
worth his salt.

Saint Patrick, of course, blessed it, the Vikings
ravaged it, the Norman colonists rebuilt its
three-metre-thick walls, Irish tribes fought over
it. Cromwell razed it.

Now even the goats which gave the place its
name Beann Gabhar, Bengore, Peak of Goats,
have gone to legend too, though east on craggier
Beann Mór, Benmore, Big Ben on Fair Head,
the agile and the patient can spot the ruttish
ruminant munching at vanilla-scented whin-
blossom down in the rock chasms cut by the
North's other terrifying Celtic nemesis, the
Grey Man pounding his once and only path
from sea to sea.

Dunseverick,
Bengore Head

Finn Mac Cool was a giant amongst men. Perhaps by today's standards he took the odd too many drams of whiskey, *uisce beatha*, distilled from the pure but peaty waters of St Colum's Rill, at Bushmills. But, an outsider by the grotesquerie of his size, who's to judge from our own times when tribal conformity has meant life, or death?

The big lad and his Scots neighbour Fingal hurled insults back and forth across the peace line of the Sea of Moyle till rumour spread that Fingal was engaged in constructing a Causeway from Staffa, to match Finn's. Mac Cool was neither coward nor fool.

When he heard the heavy step of the Scot approaching, he begged his wife Oonagh to wrap him in hectares of good Irish linen swadling clothes in a huge makeshift cradle. When Fingal hove up Finn suckled his thumb and mooed as a herd of kine. The canny Scot, his whisky wearing off, calculated on his fat and red-haired fingers that if this was the suckling, the father would be too much to handle. Mac Cool hurled a great sod which became the Isle of Man after the retreating figure, the hollow, left behind, Lough Neagh.

Top: Giant's Causeway
Left: Looking towards the Giant's
Causeway from the Stookans

Cut off by the sea on one hand and by natural moats on the other, sombre Dunluce could be reached by drawbridge or boat. Sorley Boy MacDonnell took it back from Sir John Perrott, natural son of Henry VIII, by infiltrating the castle staff, lowering a basket over the cliff's edge to haul up the rest of his cutthroats. Every age has its commandos. And there's a ghost's lair in Maeve's tower, and a grand enough tale of sweating kitchen scullions swept away in a winter's storm. To round off this tale, you've to pity the diners, deprived of boiled mutton, roast deer. Pity too the men of the overmanned Armada galleass *Girona,* drowned when their navigator mistook the Causeway's formations for the castle's. 'No tengo más que dar te', 'I have nothing more to give you', runs the poignant inscription on a salvaged ring now secure in the province's principal museum, the Ulster.

Right and *below*. Dunluce Castle

Of the little ports along the north coast, each has its postcard caption. Ballycastle has a song and a fair, winding streets, old shop fronts, a Diamond, a port and a memorial to Marconi who transmitted shipping news from Rathlin to the London futures markets. Ballintoy has a limestone harbour and a crazed house of many windows to catch each and every view, built by the artist Newton Penprase. Its whitewashed church a beacon to both sailor and worshipper.

Bushmills has salmon in its river and whiskey from this archipelago's oldest licensed place of distillation. Portballintrae, the port by the house by the beach, has boats to hire for fish or the caves at Dunluce and the Giant's Causeway. Portbraddan, tucked cold in the evening in the shadow of the west cliffs of Whitepark Bay, claims this island's smallest church, a modest effort as it's named for Gobhan, patron saint of builders.

Portbraddan

Foolish though would be the sea captain who tried to thread his skiff through the Wishing Arch to change passengers' fortunes.

The sea hollowed out caves as well as arches and from neolithic times till the Iron Age people used them as homes and stores and hideaways. Indeed the whole of Antrim's coast is rich in early archaeological evidence. Cairns and tombs dot the countryside. Crannogs prettify lakes.

Within the tombs were plain and decorated pottery shards and sometimes stylish gold. Manufactured glass beads exist. Ring forts abound, ditched and posted, some even with the traces of cobbled approach roads. The stone axe heads polished on Rathlin and at Tievebulliagh west of Cushendall were traded across the islands in a sophisticated commerce. Flint arrowhead finds are many.

Pollen and grain show which strains of wheat and barley were favoured, bone and hair indicate the domestication of goats and sheep. There must be cockle, winkle, mussel and razorshell yet to be found amongst the middens, the backbones of dab and flounder speared in the shallows, scales of grey mullet chased on to the shore in tiny bays, to be grasped, belaboured, hooked and cooked.

Below: The White Rocks
Opposite: The Wishing Arch

Portstewart, stranded in the wrong
county if you look at nature's
rather than a politician's wily
geography, once wished to be
prim. Her railway station,
necessary for any Victorian resort's
prosperity, was confined to the
outskirts. A convent school
dominates promontory, town,
harbour and lovers' sunsets.

But her strand is bracing, her
Italian ice-cream makers notable,
and in winter, students from the
university in nearby Coleraine
hunch out on to what would
otherwise be empty, wind-
whistled, spume-wet streets.

Top and bottom:
Portstewart

The Earl Bishop's is the road across Binevenagh. Buzzard, hen harrier, merlin and raven survive here. Even maybe the secretive red grouse. Siskin breed, crossbill tear at the spruce trees' cones. The native brown trout never made it to the reservoir lake, just supermarket rainbows, bred for put and take. Below, Benone strand sweeps west to the Foyle's mouth at Magilligan's sand-spit where, in 1812, by English overtures, a round tower was built to designs impregnable to guns at Mortella, Corsica. They called it a Martello, getting neither spelling nor pronunciation right. The chain of towers were as protection against another Corsican device, Napoleon and his French ships, plus the increasingly daring and increasingly revolting American colonists. Another was built across the Foyle at Greencastle, the twins with their artillery and artillery men stationed to defend with crossfire the approaches to the rich walled city then called Londonderry.

Top: Binevenagh Lake
Bottom: Looking towards
Magilligan from Binevenagh

Frederick Augustus Hervey, being only an aristo's
younger son, took, as to the fashion of the day for
younger and relatively impecunious siblings, to holy
orders and obtained the preferment of chaplain to
George III which of course demonstrated how
un-impecunious he really was. On the death of his
brother he became Earl of Bristol, and with an
income of £10,000 a year from the bishopric of
Derry and an equal sum from his inheritance, he set
about the Grand Tour with an enthusiasm so

Mussenden Temple,
Downhill

constant he rarely allowed himself time to visit in
Ireland. Still, when he was at Downhill he
constructed both Catholic and Protestant churches,
elegant in their simplicity, and if the Continent's
hoteliers wished to change the name of their
establishments to Bristol to attract – or to imply
they had attracted – his custom, didn't he add
suitably to the sum of our amusement by staging
plump clerics' races, on foot and by horse across to
Downhill's soft strand. The winners gained livings at

his disposal. His windswept palace is but a shell now,
its gateways the more impressive. The Battalion Gate
is all Doric column, bishop's mitre, horned beasts
and a statue of Diana. Each Lion Gate's pier is
topped not by a lion, but by the arcanely named
ounce, a snow leopard. The isolation of the nearby
temple built for cousin Frideswide Mussenden
suggests more cozenage than cousinry.

Right: Bluebells, Downhill
Below: Waterfall, Downhill
Opposite (top): Woodland, Downhill

So, right at the cliff's edge, sixty metres above the sea, is this pleasingly symmetrical rotunda of what is now constantly referred to as the Mussenden Temple. On the temple's interior frieze the idiosyncratically chosen inscription in Latin is from Lucretius, but the poet Dryden has left a suitably intriguing translation:

'Tis pleasant, safely to behold from shore,
The rolling ship, and hear the tempest's roar.

Ho ho, no doubt, went the Earl Bishop, laughing into the cliff-top breeze, calling for more malmsey wine and flourishing his duelling pistols, now incongruously and piously displayed in the chapterhouse of St Columb's Church of Ireland Cathedral.

It was designed first as a summer library in the style of the Temple of Vesta in Tivoli, but Mrs Mussenden died before completion of the charming rotunda. On occasion the good bishop, whose liberal as well as eclectic ideas disturbed many who could not afford to show disagreement, encouraged Catholics to hold mass in the room beneath.

East and north are the Scottish Isles; west, Inishowen, the sunsets and the Foyle. Closer by, waterfalls and walks can evoke some of the good bishop's joys.

Right: Binevenagh
Below: Panorama across reclaimed
lands and Lough Foyle

In the wintry distance, the River Roe, far far from its distant source near the peak of Mullaghaneany in the lonely Sperrins, snakes west into its own estuary under the railway bridge and into Lough Foyle and the setting sun. Far up in Binevenagh's silence, maybe a distant train, crossing the Roe's bridge, pulls the mind's focus to down there where the waders come at low tide and retreat obligingly towards the watcher at high. Curlew, dunlin, godwit, knot, oystercatcher, plover, spotted and un-spotted redshank, little stint. Rooting in salt marsh, mud flat, mussel bed, shingle ridge. Widgeon in their thousands nuzzle at the eel grass. Gadwall, mallard, pintail, teal and shoveller dodge and dip amongst them.

Whooper and Bewick's swan winter-graze on the reclaimed meadow polder levels. The anserine thousands, Greenland white-fronts, pale-bellied brents, greylag and sometimes pink foot and barnacle make up the honking goose skeins overhead, then swing, loose altitude, brake flat-footedly to become eel-grass foraging flocks. Snow bunting, finch, pipit, sparrow and large flocks strip stubble. Raptors – buzzard, kestrel, merlin, peregrine, sparrowhawk, even gyrfalcon – wait, high in the sky. Gales blow in storm petrel, Arctic and great skua, plus exotic visitors of perplexing rarity. Great-crested and Slavonian grebe, black-throated, great-northern and red-throated diver ride the waves.

And what of the Celts who invaded and colonised Ireland before the fifth-century Christian missionaries, the ninth-century Vikings, the twelfth-century Welsh-Normans, brutal Cromwell and the seventeenth-century London Guilds and planters? Delineated now by cautious post-modern anthropologists, the Celts – spreading across Europe and north Africa from the Balkans – are only those who are known to have been so described by their contemporaries. And what of the Milesian colonialists before them, who defeated the Dé Danaan, who repulsed the Formorii invaders? The sixth-century monks who, slowly, scribed the Book of Invasions, accommodated fable, metaphor and moral instruction as they combined loose skeins of pagan song and story, matched them with mountain peak, river valley, enigmatic piled stones and geometric circles and wove them into cloth fit for their vision of a noble Christian race. Suffice it to say of the North's history that the Dé Danaan – so versed in the magicals of battle that they were invisible when they stood sideways to the west wind – became a people of such lambent lustrous beauty that they could not bear to look upon their own reflection and thus they banished themselves to their own underworld and the entrance to that underworld was at the mouth of the River Foyle.

Mad Sweeney, Suibhne Geilt, the seventh-
century king of Dál Riata, turned to a bird by
Saint Ronan, his seat at Dunseverick, knew
that

> the bushy leafy oaktree
> is highest in the wood

for under the old Brehon law system by which
trees were, quite rightly, protected and
conserved, the oak was listed as the most noble
of trees and the penalty for felling one was a
seoit, being one and a quarter set, each set
equalling a fine of two milch cows. Cutting off
an oak branch without permission cost the
perpetrator a one-year-old heifer; cutting off a
fork raised the ante to a two-year-old heifer.

River Foyle

Craigavon Bridge, Derry

The oak had another great resonance. For the letters of the old ogham runes had – in an *alphabet végétal* – bccn given the names of the great trees so central was their essence for the old gods, and that which was the ogham letter D was *dair, doire* in contemporary Irish for an oakwood. So, Saint Colum when he came, knew what he was about. He operated with a sensitivity, and a pragmatism, towards the old gods and their laws not always evinced by later generations of Christian prosletysers and colonists, here or far afield.

When he built his first church in the lee of a pagan-cult oakwood, which was to give his settlement its name Doire (which you can pronounce near enough as Derry), on a hill top on the west bank of the Foyle, he made sure his masons left the trees standing and called it now a sacred Christian grove.

Of course, all that is written of the Irish oak may not be true, though it has been designated Ireland's national tree.

There are pedants who would argue that though

few English spiders web the oak hammer beam roof of London's Westminster Hall, it does not prove the wood came from Ireland. The same spoilsport antiquaries would also cast doubt on the accepted Irish oak provenance for the roof of Salisbury Cathedral and that of the chapel of the King's College, Cambridge. However, even they will leave the carved stalls of Rouen's cathedral and timbers of Amsterdam's Stadt House as Irish.

Above: Looking down Shipquay Street to Derry's walls
Opposite: Sculpture, Derry

When academics researched the plans of towns
established on the eastern seaboard of America by
the first European colonists – many of whom
embarked from Derry's quays in the eighteenth
century – they discovered a remarkable similarity
between those of the city of Philadelphia and the
first street plans of Derry. Further research shows
both, in turn, to be of a remarkable similarity to
those for the French Renaissance city of Vitry-le-
François, on the River Marne, east of Paris, finished
in 1560. A central square is reached by a cross shape
of streets from a rectangular walled defence in the
style of a Roman military fort.

Vitry was razed. The city of brotherly love has
changed, but Derry, and its stout siege canon walls,
survives. Gates echo the North's iconography;
Ferryquay's is embellished with effigies of those who
saved the city for Protestant William against
Catholic James in 1689. An annual rite prescribes
auto-da-fé for one deemed that siege's traitor,
Lundy, in ephemeral effigy. Outside the walls a gable
proclaims the 'Free Derry' of more recent times.
When the first transatlantic aviatrix Amelia Earhart
landed nearby in 1932 she thought this was France.
Just by Vitry-le-François perhaps?

The great sea loughs of Foyle, Swilly, Mulroy and Sheep Haven, each with its legendary sea monster, cut ragged swathes between the mountains of the north-west, and inland, the trouty rivers snake up narrow valleys, passes for the lonesome roads of Donegal, where towns and, even villages, are few and many still have miles to go before they sleep.

Some say the Grianan of Aileach is the sun palace of Aileach, built a few kilometres west of Derry in the last centuries BC for a royal line of sun-worshippers. In its centre, argue the romantics, the priest would have sacrificed whilst the worshippers watched from the tiered circular terraces. Certainly the enclosing stone wall, 5 metres high, 4 metres thick and at 23 metres in diameter, atop a 240-metre hill, is impressive enough for any imaginings, fey, erotic, sporting or astrological. There is an architectural presence not quite diminished by insensitive restoration, and the traveller passes on bewildered, yet again, by how little this island knows of its ancient past. More accessible, in foxed or shiny tomes, is its more recent contentious history.

Above: Near Muckish
Opposite (*top*): Grianan of Aileach

Right: Lough Swilly
Below: Ballymastocker Bay, near Portsalon

Beauty is in the eye of the traveller. The crescent of
golden sand, an offshore breeze slicing the tops off
the rolling breakers the way a country barber would,
with a cutthroat razor, once have scalped the white
whiskers off the wind-reddened face of a mass-going
farmer . . . or the way, when they still called a good
barman a 'curate', he'd – his striped shirt sleeves
held back with the elastic thingummies the brother
sent him back from Amerikay, his grey-black apron
shining the tops of his cracked and beer-tanned
shoes – have scooped the froth off a pint with a
knife whose chipped ivory handle was bronzed to
the colour of chewin' tobacco.

A cottage sparkles. The heather springs back after
the walker's boot passes on. There are bilberries
between the rocks, and mountain avens, and, in
the season that's in it, dusty blue vernal squill. The
air would do you a power of good. Not much
west between Lough Swilly's Ballymastocker and
Boston, bar the Fanad and Rosguill peninsulas and
a few thousand or so miles of rolling Atlantic.

But today's Donegal is a sum of its pasts. In the
dusty academic libraries of this island's two capital
cities, foxed a little but leather bound and heavy,
sit, their pages unturned for many a year, the
dutifully minuted pages of a government's
deliberations. The Report of the Commissioners of
Inquiry into the State of the Irish Fisheries – which
met in various towns in the county of Donegal in
the month of January 1836, and which Report was
presented to both Houses of Parliament by
Command of His Majesty – makes salutary reading;
selections from the evidence of Lieutenants
M'Gladery, Stevens, Wall and Penfold of the Coast
Guard being particularly pertinent: 'Cod, Ling,
Conger-eel, Skate, Haddock, Turbot, Sole, Plaice
and various other fish are taken off Mulroy. The
only fishing craft in use are these wretched curaghs
of which there are but seven or eight fitted with
small spillards or hand lines. The fisherman who
has a small spot of land is in better circumstances
than one who has no land, being able to raise
potatoes for his family. The rent of potato-land is
nearly double that paid for other land . . .

'The people construct what they call a tram by sewing together a number of sheets and blankets; by this contrivance considerable quantities of small fish are taken. The poor people have nothing to cover them at night when their bedclothes are used in this way. The general habits and morals of the fishermen in this district are much the same as working tradesmen and agricultural labourers; but their circumstances are not so good, owing to the precarious employment fishing gives . . . I do not think the use of ardent spirits prevails to any great extent . . .

Right: Dunfanaghy
Below: The Atlantic Drive looking over Sheep Haven

Dunfanaghy

'There are eight or ten families who are supported by subscription, the heads of the families having perished at sea. There is not a magistrate within thirteen miles of this harbour; and when two fishermen dispute, the quarrel is not settled without fighting, in which all join in on either side, with sticks; many are thus disabled from fishing during the remainder of the time for which the fisher continues . . .

'In Guidore there are no loan funds, benefit societies, or savings banks; fishermen are too poor to make investments; and since the extinction of the loan fund of the late Fishery Board, fishing has been entirely knocked up . . .

Above: Horn Head from Bloody Foreland
Right: Errigal

'It is lamentable to see thousands of people starving here at times, when the harbour and the whole coast generally is teeming with fish – Mackerel, Herrings etc. If stores of salt where placed at Cruit and Guidore, to be sold at a reasonable rate, they would also be of immense benefit to the country.

'The fishermen are, from the very circumstances in which they are placed, prone to every evil: – idleness brings a multitude of other bad habits with it: – but I think them capable of great improvement, and willing and anxious to receive it. They, in general, drink hard; and their circumstances are miserable beyond description. Very few of them are without land: – if they were they would inevitably starve. Those who have no land are wretchedly poor, but the reason is obvious; they have neither fishing gear nor boats. Their wives and daughters spin wool, knit stockings . . .

'The earnings of a thrifty fisherman would be sufficient to maintain a family, if there were means of fishing.

'There never has been any mode of supporting the families of fishermen unable to work, not even when the fishery was at its height; and there being now no fishery, though there are plenty of fish, very many are destitute. Fishermen without land have to work by rule, three days in the week in payment of cabin and turf rent: they are fishing on the other days, when the weather permits; otherwise they are depending on the bounty of neighbours. They suffer much hardship from insufficiency of fuel . . .'

Gweedore

Here endeth the lesson. A hard one to forget, a sermon to awaken spectres as the traveller tootles past Dawros Head, a place then spelt as Daurus, where the good lieutenant was pleased to report on the excellence of the fishermen's morals and on their great forbearance notwithstanding the drowning of twenty-four men during the herring season. Best still, on holiday, to remember smiles of miles in a county seemingly entirely signposted in 'Drives' around the headlands for the obedient city slickers across from Belfast for the golf, a trout, a pint, a sweater and the long drive home.

The 160-kilometre Inishowen Drive with the miracle of the loaves and fishes carved on Clonca Cross near Culdaff where Bonnie Prince Charlie landed. Then on to Ireland's most northerly point Malin Head, with Fort Dunree's sunken gold, west. Elegant Ramelton, Fanad Head, farmed shellfish and salmon-rich Mulroy Bay. The Atlantic Drive, Dunfanaghy, Sheep Haven, Horn Head, Tory Island offshore, Bloody Foreland, Gweedore, Dunlewey, the charmed gardens of Glenveagh, The Rosses with Burtonport for Aran Island and Dunglow their capital. The tidal inlet at Maas.

Over a century and a half ago the coast's shellfish – clam, cockle, goose barnacle, mussel, oyster, razorshell and scallop – were abundant in their neglected natural estuarial beds. Cod, haddock, skate and turbot swam the unpolluted seas, safe from bobbing curraghs too frail to venture past the shoals' edges. Now million-pound trawlers must hunt as far as Biscay's tuna and the Grand Banks' halibut. Salmon cages sway, mussel ropes bob, in inshore waters.

Left: Evening fishing near Dunglow
Bottom: Maas

Up above Ardara, where now the tourist buys
pints and knitted woollen socks and there's
hardly a fresh fish to be found on the menu,
once the passes of the Blue Stack Mountains
were shared with about equal degrees of
discomfort by redcoats and highwaymen; the
one barracking, marching, drinking; the other
dividing the spoils, ambuscading, drinking.

Now, back from the coast, off from the
tourist villages, even pubs are few. No one
calls for the telling of the rosary at closing
time any more.

Sheep graze, abandoned railway lines – their ways no longer permanent – track into the distance, streams tumble, a lough's surface riffles, and cloud, mist and mountain meld. Sometimes, in a valley, empty bar and abandoned cottage, the plangent scent of a hearth's ghost smoke asks questions never to be answered. Even, one supposes, then back in the redcoat's time there'd have been an oul' wan in the pub who'd say – in exchange for a pint – that in exchange for the almost perpetual dampness of the climate, in compensation, isn't there almost always a rainbow?

Top and *bottom*: Glencolumbcille
Opposite (*top*): Port
Opposite (*bottom*): Ardara Falls

There is a path that runs up over Carrigan
Head, past Lough O Mulligan and on to the
dizzying 300-metre drop to the sea at
Bunglass. With nerve and a fine day there's
more of a challenge still to come: One Man's
Pass along the ledge, the sea 540 metres
below to the left and much the same fall
down the escarpment to the right. A single
farmstead crouches in the distant valley.
Beyond, for the brave, is Slieve League's
summit 590 metres above the sea.

One bed-and-breakfast story places Bonnie Prince Charlie hiding in these valleys, another offers Dylan Thomas. Bronze Age cairns and dolmens break from amongst the heathers. The lichened stones of church ruins lie abandoned amongst the sedges. There are ring forts away north and Rathlin O'Birne, the island offshore, served refuge for a saint called Hugh Mac Bric. New bungalows scatter by the roadside and up the slopes, offending the tourist's idyll.

Slieve League

When the Commission was inquiring into
the state of fishing, mention was made of
great whales entering the bay at Inver each
year and of a certain Mr Nesbit, to whom
the Irish government had given a large sum
to encourage the fishing for whales there.
But none present at Killybegs on 14 January
1836 could give account of it.

In the graveyard of the ruined church there
is a stone to Thomas Nesbit, born in the
village in 1730, inventor of the gun-harpoon
for whaling.

Saint Patrick expelled not only the snakes from Ireland but the evil spirits which infested a cavern on the island on Lough Derg, east of Donegal town. Thus, in the middle ages, from right across professed Christian Europe, the rich and the penitent came (or sent their poorer relatives as proxies) as pilgrims. Even now, as the twentieth century ends, in the pilgrimage season, from June to mid-August, the barefoot come still, taking water, bread and black tea – the last a stimulant the good saint never had – for three days of prayer and penitential exercise.

Above: Teelin
Left: Coastline near Killybegs
Opposite (*top*): Sheep near Teelin

Tyrone amongst the bushes was the county of the O'Neills, the last of the old Irish families to hold out against the English invaders till they lost all at the battle of Benburb.

But cast about now and this is still a county whose both real and presented history is caught in the parameters of the past.

From Plumbridge to Castlederg traces of what the subservient who knew their place once called the 'oul' dacency' abound and can be read in the copses and tumbled boughs glimpsed by the curious through the gaps in the crumbling walls of the old estates which still divide up much of the best land.

At country road bends, once proud gateposts, now bent and cracked, sag where a lorry brushed, where once not one single person would have dared lean. Sometimes the big house just crumbled, sometimes built on one whim, it was abandoned for another. Sometimes, it was torched by insurgents, or for insurance, in the twenties.

Criss-crossed wrought-iron gates are held together with binder twine, fencing wire and new-fangled neon-coloured cords which look like a farm-hand's raffia. A half-bag of cement, now set to stone, lying nearby, points to a struggle for appearances now finally abandoned.

Woodland near
Plumbridge

Leaves deepen in lubricious drifts across the
antique and winding avenue, ivy clogging its
pillared beeches. Rough board and fertiliser bag
hold closed the leaning gatehouse window. And
much can be read too from those gatehouses,
once policing the grey granite line, symbolic
sentry boxes between aristocrat (real or pretend)
and the people, a boundary marked by
gatehouses as a dog fox sprays its pheromone, tree
to tree. But sometimes the gatehouse was but a
frippery, built to a new fashion. Sometimes the
old house had to rest in the old style, its owner
unable to afford a complete make-over of the
sprawling demesne. Sometimes, when the big
house was rebuilt, only the gatehouse tells of its
original style. Now, sometimes, beyond, are forest
parks, picnic sites, signposted panoramas.

Above: Woodland near
Castlederg
Left: Sloughan waterfall

Right: Ulster History Park
Below: Fungi, Gortin Country Park
Bottom: Gortin

A catalogue of the lodges can, if you so wish, be an album of despair. Or of pity. Or of curiosity, of cap-doffing, of the politics of envy or of resentment, of the rights of man, of joy.

How many, of a Sunday morn, as the wrought-iron floor-grill over the antique and sunken heating pipe squeaks its once weekly expansion, in tiny, cold and sparsely beautiful planters' gothick village churches, now sing in holy praise with Mrs Cecil F. Alexander, a nineteenth-century bishop's wife late of Londonderry, who gave the children this verse to sing from a number in the Church of Ireland hymnal? 'All Things Bright and Beautiful'?

> The rich man in his castle,
> The poor man at his gate,
> God made them high or lowly,
> And ordered their estate.

There's a stained-glass window in St Columb's Cathedral, in the Maiden City, to the same bishop's lady who also wrote 'There is a Green Hill Far Away' and the Christmas carol 'Once in Royal David's City'.

No stained-glass though in the spartan dry-stone monks' cell, oratory and round tower in Gortin's Ulster History Park, all built as near as dammit, down to a deliberately replicated mason's mistake, in perfect reproduction of those once hallowed icons of Ireland's ecclesiastical past. Nearby, the Ulster-American Folk Park offers the old world as it was when emigrants left, and the new world as they first built it.

Gortin Glen Forest Park, thick with conifer, spans a splendid gorge on the side of Mullaghcarn Mountain and forests and forest parks dot the county far and wide. At vast Baronscourt, seat still of the Dukes of Abercorn, the lodges come straight from a picture book. At Drum Manor the lodges are gothick, at Favour Royal Tudor, at Parkanaur grandiose.

Above: Gortin Country Park
Left: Gortin Lakes

Top: Tyrone landscape near
Omagh
Bottom and *opposite*:
Glenelly valley

North of Baronscourt's big demesne, the Glenelly river, having joined with the Owenkillew upstream, joins with the Strule to become the Mourne which, in turn, runs north to mix with the Finn beyond Strabane to become the Foyle flowing towards the underwater trapdoor of the Dé Danaan. But the Glenelly's delights are back upstream above, between the disturbing emptiness of the Sperrin peaks – Mullaghasturrakeen, Mullaghcloga, Dart, Sawel, Meenard, Oughtvabeg, Oughtmore, Mullaghneaney, Mullaghmore and White, fellow travellers, mostly, with the county boundary with Derry to the north and Mullaghcarn, Craignamaddy, Carnanelly and Mullaghturk and Slieve Gallion to the south.

Ulster is not a country of sheep bells. Carved and sliced, the hills and valleys, on a windless day, are silent. Just the clicking as the metal in your engine cools, contracting beneath the map spread across the still-warm car bonnet. There's a brace of history parks south and west, a scattering of planters' guilds' towns north and east, and enough forest parks to shake a car rug at all around.

The literary should know that playwright Brian Friel comes from Omagh, satirist Flann O'Brien from Strabane. If you can whistle 'Red Sails in the Sunset', or 'South of the Border', comforting to know that lyricist Jimmy Kennedy was an Omagh man too.

Giant's graves and fairy thorns, a saint's well,
a wronged maid's leap, the friar's buck lep,
Saint Patrick's this and that? The countryside
is thick with them. Most forgotten; most
unexplained; some guessed at. Turn the sun-
yellowed-bordered pages of an old guide
book and set to trace the most curious and
the traveller ends in bramble thicket or
peering over a stone ditch, primrose
speckled, topped with rusty barbed wire.

Above: Snow in the Sperrins
Right: Beaghmore stone circles
Opposite (*top*): Keerogue cross,
near Clogher

Next comes the nervy confrontation with a loose herd of Friesian cows, heavy heads swinging, grass-chewing suspended in some bovine air of near menace. Citing their farming antecedents, some will then climb the ditch, ducking and squeezing with less than grace between the rusty strands, dragging old, long and curious staples from the lichened ash-plant post. Others feign interest in an unnamed vetch, or curse a now revealed cowpat whilst our hero and heroine edge towards the ring of part-tumbled stones, half-sensing imagined underground vibrations from the presence of the old gods below the grass tufts.

Few are laid out in the tight phallic rhythms of Beaghmore. None are now the perfect circles of schoolbook mathematics. Nor are they ever the massive uprights of a picture-book Stonehenge. Here an uneven boulder stone has tumbled; here someone rolled back the grave's capstone; here another, inexplicably, has just vanished. Two sit down the hill, another further up, out of any precise alignment.

Enough to wonder how they came here, rolled and dragged for days and leagues from another distant place. Who paid the workforce? Or who coerced them? For how long? A week? A day? Three summers? Did they come willingly to this church, if that is what it was? Did laggards loll, nibbling wild mushrooms in the ditch? Who dragged the stone for the old rugged cross from there to here?

Ireland's first peoples had wriggly eels to eat, if they could catch them. And trout to tickle, and sea trout and salmon to dam and spear. And in the lakes, fatter trout in many variations, and their distant relative the charr in even greater variations, and their even more distant and primitive cousins, the pollan.

Carapaced freshwater crayfish were caught and crunched and sucked dry beside these and many bubbling waters. But the River Mourne's great heavy mussels offer not nourishment but the lustrous pearl. Infrequently.

Top and *bottom*: River Mourne

Beragh Leap Bridge

Monks and monasteries, that great evolutionary
step the knowledge of the written, printed word
on their side, introduced new species, dammed
ponds and bred carp and tench and pike,
developed and managed and appropriated the eel
and salmon weirs. The big houses followed suit,
and by their ponds too, the still summer
morning's calm would have been broken by the
flurry of jack pike in the tepid shallows.

The lake at Augher Castle, once Spur Royal,
once the Castle Keep, and exquisitely built in the
form of an Elizabethan tower house for Sir
Thomas Ridgeway in 1613, would have been no
exception even before the picturesque
transformation to gothick effected in 1832 by a
Sligo man called William Warren, who added the
amusingly unnecessary castellations and the
affectations of false and joky bartizans.

And Augher itself? The name of a cheese? A
village now sitting crossways to its main traffic, a
pretty enough Protestant chapel of ease, a railway
station lost to progress which once puffed
uneconomically along its main street, a literary
memory of novelist and commentator William
Carleton who lived up the road a bit and a
mention in the litany and rote of a children's rap
from the railway's timetable for Augher and
Clogher and Fivemiletown.

Augher Castle

On Enniskillen's west shore stands the fairytale
Watergate, fashioned on the site of a castle taken
and lost and won back again from the hereditary
Fermanagh chieftains – the Maguires. Lisnaskea's
governor, John Dowdall, took it first by siege in
1594 and on 15 May 1607 William Cole,
captain of the (English) King's Long Boats, was
appointed the castle's captain too. East of the
island town, on the mainland, atop a massive
soaring Doric column perched at the summit of
Fort Hill, now a prim Victorian park, stands the
stone statue, cavalry sabre in left hand, of

General Sir Galbraith Lowry Cole, a soldier whose preferment was much assisted, no doubt, by his marriage to the Duke of Wellington's unwanted betrothed during the Peninsular War, 1808–14. Incised letters at the column's base record his battles there, triumphant up the castle's cobbled ramp in lovely dazzling Olivenza on the southern sun-blistered plains of Spain's Extremadura. No unseemly memory here of his role at Vinegar Hill, crushing the men of '98.

Sir William Cole, the black-haired one, raised a regiment of horse in Devon to fight in the Irish wars. For his pains, and no doubt those of his soldiers and their horses too, he was rewarded with estates by this lough shore and the governorship of the town during its rejection of the 1641 rising.

His grandson Sir Michael fled the country during the Williamite War (so much for Derry, Aughrim, Enniskillen and the Boyne) only to return and have his son John have a son who became Lord Mountflorence and improved the buildings of the town and the roads about. And thus the Coles prospered. Mountflorence's son became Earl of Enniskillen and the earl's second son was Galbraith. In effect the town was the family's fiefdom, its corporation but an exercise in deference.

Opposite (top): River Erne at Killyhevlin
Left: The Watergate, Enniskillen

And, so it went, all about the county of Fermanagh as the planters came, consolidated, intermarried. The Archdales from Stafford built Castle Archdale, saw it burned, entered politics, refused bribes, hunted down priests, became generals. The Atkinsons were gifted the manor of Coole and sold it to the Champions who built Castle Coole and then sold it to the Corrys from Dumfries who intermarried with the Coles, begat the Earls of Belmore and rebuilt Castle Coole to James Wyatt's elegant Palladian designs after the Williamite War. The Coles, by now Earls of Enniskillen, built Georgian Florence Court, commissioned its arcaded pavilions, its stunning plasterwork.

The Aughenlecks, planters from Scotland, married Corrys and produced a field marshal.

The Montgomerys from Normandy produced
another. The Brookes obtained Colebrooke
under Cromwell and produced yet another. Lord
Burley built Castle Balfour and sold it to the
Edinburgh Crichtons who acquired Crom Castle
by marriage, became Earls of Erne and gave
employment to both Captain Boycott and the
father of novelist Shan F. Bullock.

Opposite: Florence Court House
Below: Colebrooke House

Dean Swift called it the longest lake
in Ireland and the gentry sailed from
Crom for pleasure, a paddle steamer
plied from Wattlebridge to
Enniskillen, steamers carried
passengers and freight from Belleek
to Enniskillen and on to Belfast and
Newry. Picnics on the islands
became the thing and chaps from
the big houses penned monographs,
concerning graveyard inscriptions,
churches and carved stones, for
antiquarian journals. Vanity
publishers printed family histories at
no mean cost. Titled naturalists
annotated flowers and a Cole had a
species of charr named after him:
Salvelinus alpinus colii.

Top: Devenish Island, Lower
Lough Erne
Bottom: Looking towards
Devenish Island from Dead
Man's Lane
Opposite: Devenish Tower

The Brookes spawned Charles Stewart Parnell and the province's hardest line Prime Minister, Sir Basil Brooke, who boasted of employing no Catholics. On the shores of the Erne's Lower Lough, almost all of which can be seen from the top of Mahoo Cliffs on the edge of Navar Forest Park, a park rich in the particular of bog-land vegetation, more planter families planted. The Bloomfields established Belleek's world famous pottery. The Blennerhassets built Cleenish Castle and Castlecaldwell village. The Caldwells served in the armies of the Empress Maria Theresa of Austria. The London Gores became Viscounts of Belleisle.

The Humes, controllers of Scotland, built Castle Hume on the south shore of the Lower Lough; castle and servants were torched by the Maguires on Christmas 1641. The Humes were spared . . . Robert Hamilton took 600 hectares at the plantation. His son Malcolm, who built stout and corbelled Monea Castle not far from Tully's, became an archbishop and fathered Lewis Baron of Deserf and Laird of Nabben in Sweden, whose son in turn, Gustavus, governor of Enniskillen, was raised to the peerage as Viscount Boyne for services to King Billy when serving as a general at the Battle of the Boyne; commanding the Inniskillings, no doubt.

Left: Bog cotton
Below: Lower Lough Erne looking towards
Belleek

Indeed the island town's four hills tell the whole story. On Fort Hill, prim and Protestant-looking on the mainland, east, is the boul general at the head of a long spiral staircase. Below is Mount Lourdes Catholic girls' school. Across the river the old Orange Hall. Along the winding main street, past the courthouse, the *Impartial Reporter*, implacable in its politics.

Once it employed columnist Barney Maglone who came to work in a Roman toga. Next comes the Town Hall, beside the Diamond where, till the mid-1940s the Lowry-Corrys, Earls of Belmore, arrived by hansom cab, once each month, top hats in place, to have their hair cut in Johnston's barber shop. High up in the Town Hall's walls are niches for stone statues of the men of the Royal Inniskilling Dragoons and the Royal Inniskilling Fusiliers.

Below and *opposite*: Lower Lough Erne

Inside the Town Hall is a plaque to Captain Oates of the Dragoons, epitome of a particular bravery easily mocked today. With Scott returning from the doomed south-polar expedition of 1912, he walked out of his tent into the blizzard, a sacrifice for others. The next hill west offers the three main churches, Catholic St Michael's, the Methodist chapel and St Macartin's Church of Ireland Cathedral with its Inniskilling regimental flags and its bell cast from a cannon fired at the Battle of the Boyne.

In the west wall of the nave a stone commemorating William Pokrich, who died in 1628, is inscribed with Cromwell's dying words:

GRAUNT ME MERCIFUL SAVIOUR THAT NOW DEATH HAS SHUT UP THE EYES OF MY BODY YET THE EYES OF MY SOULE MAY STILL BEHOLD AND LOKKE UPPON THEE AND WHEN DEATH HATH TAKEN AWAY THE USE OF MY TOUNG YET MY HEART MAY CRY AND SAY LORD INTO THY HANDES I COMMEND MY SOULE LORD JESUS RECEIVE MY SPIRIT.

Between the island's two hills, by the loughside, the old Buttermarket now offers history sanitised. West, those fairytale turrets of the Watergate Castle, additions to a fort of the warring Maguires, fiefs till the planter came, houses – with no irony – both the museum to the planter regiments (King William's pretorian guard at the Battle of the Boyne) and replicas of Celtic icons. On the fourth hill, west again, Portora Royal School, founded by Charles I. Portora, Crom, Tully, Archdale, Crevenish, Caldwell – and Enniskillen – castles forged the planters' ring of steel.

Left and *below*: Crom Castle

Right: Orchid
Below: Lough Melvin
Opposite (*top*): Janus stone on Boa
Island, Lower Lough Erne
Opposite (*bottom*): Upper Lough Erne

This is a county of curious legends: they codify ogham stones on mountain tops, crannogs in forgotten loughs, space ships (AD 749) recorded in the Annals of Ulster compiled at Belleisle, Philip of the Battle-Axe's fourteenth-century inland navy of white-sailed ships, the stones collected by Lough Scate's legendary giant whose tale echoes Finn Mac Cool's causeway; Finn's hounds turned to mountains, Big Dog, Little Dog, by a witch; the white horse carved into the side of Benaughlin Mountain. And the mystical monstrous pig snouting its way, sea to sea, from

Bundrowes to Lough Melvin, from Melvin to Newry, leaving in its wake the Black Pig's Dyke.

Few though so curious as the circumstances in Lough Melvin where the waters hold salmon, brown trout, sea trout, and Gray's charr and three further distinct salmonoid trout: the sonaghan, *Salmo trutta nigripinnis*, silver-sided with black fins and black and red spots; the gillaroo, *Salmo trutta stomachius*, golden with orange spots; the ferox, *Salmo trutta ferox*, fierce-mouthed, less spotted.

A master typographer worked on the stones in Galoon Island's graveyards, his lettering beautiful, precise, inventive. But the stones have another particularity – almost all are carved with skull and crossbone, coffin, bell and other arcane devices of beyond the grave. On Boa Island the region's Celtic head cult reaches its apogee in its two-faced Janus figure – one looking back to the old year, one forward to the new. Few Irish scholars, prim souls, publish photographs of its priapic side, as, till recently, few acknowledged the obvious lubricity of the female figure, adjoined with saints and bishops, in the crude reconstruction of White Island's church.

Macha, whose name the city of Armagh took to name its hill, was the beautiful and strong fertility goddess of the Celts, luring the unwary into the woods, binding them tightly with leather thongs, taking them roughly under the forest canopy, seducing them to build her a palace at nearby Navan. Her wealthy husband a widower, boasting of her prowess, bid that she could outrun any man or horse in Ulster. Though pregnant and her time upon her, she raced, and won, and died cursing giving birth to 'emain' twins as she did. A goddess dies. So, long live god. And Patrick came, a fifth-century opportunist politician–saint and built on legend.

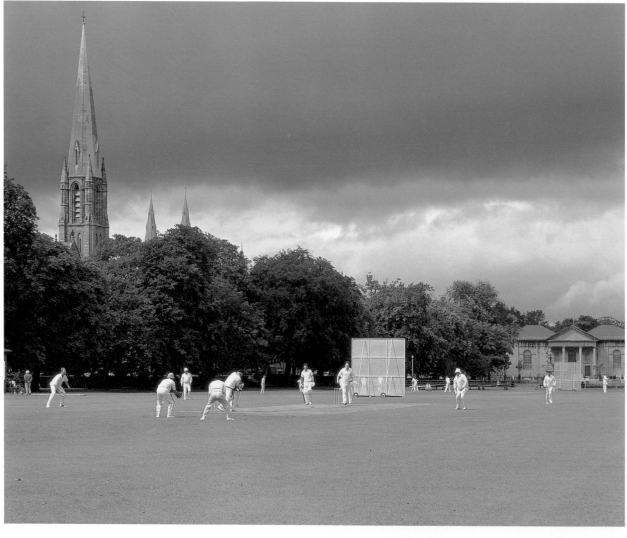

He built churches and the city prospered. And come the late eighteenth century, Francis Johnston, a local architect who gave so many of Dublin's buildings their style, worked wonders with the yellow, pink and red tones of the local sandstone. The Protestants built and rebuilt and built again where one of Patrick's churches was. Some say a statue by the crypt is of the fragrant flagrant Macha. Another, sour-faced, can be Patrick if you wish. Across a valley, in the soaring Catholic St Patrick's, hang the red hats of cardinal archbishops.

Opposite (top): St Patrick's Cathedral, Armagh
Opposite (bottom): Cricket green, Armagh

Narrow streets spiral down from Protestant St Patrick's where the elegance which Johnston lent has been much modified. And in its library is a copy, annotated in the good Dean Jonathan's own hand, of his much misunderstood *Gulliver's Travels*. During autumnal flirtations at Markethill, he composed his satirical pamphlet, *A Modest Proposal*, aping those who propose radical solutions to national crises. The eating of children, he suggests, would bring about a solution, both effective and profitable, to national poverty. Then as today.

Above (top): St Patrick's Chapel, Armagh
Above (bottom): Georgian door, Armagh

Swift was fond of the ladies. And also of gardens. He loved Quilca in Cavan and Loughall and deep in Armagh's orchard country, at Markethill, in the summer of 1728 he found opportunities to combine both of his enthusiasms. Anne Acheson sought literary attentions, her husband Sir Arthur, Sheriff of Armagh, MP for Westmeath, was a stern fellow whom she would soon leave. The gardens were pretty enough but Swift was often out and about, bantering with the labourers, devising walks and outdoor privies, between times flattering her ladyship with versified scatological 'libels'.

He came in summer but stayed for the apple pruning, writing to his friend Sheridan for 'a Periwig, and a new riding Gown and Cassock', as well as 'a dozen Guineas'. His deanish duties at Dublin's Christchurch could be deferred till the archbishop's obligatory Christmas visit. There was quadrille to be played into the wee small hours with m'Lady Anne. Pamphlets to be written deploring the forced emigration of the Presbyterians to the American colonies.

Left: Armagh apple blossom
Opposite (*top*): Apple harvest in Armagh

Below and *opposite*: Navan

Nothing but rubble and Swift's walks remain of that
actual original planter's house at Gosford, Markethill,
which welcomed him. Just as nothing now remains
but a great evocative mound of Macha's palace at
Navan where, five thousand years ago, she ran her
hospice and where the Red Branch Knights, night
after night, remembered the bravery of Cuchulainn,
in their own particular Camelot. Centuries later
another cult ringed the mound with a splendid cone
of concentric circles of great wooden posts, the
central one half a metre in diameter, thirteen metres
high, creating a vast house of governance and
worship. The spaces between the posts were filled
with weathered limestone to the height of a man's
head. Then they, or others, burnt it down and
stacked the mound with brush and sod.

There was the skull of a Barbary ape at Navan, and human skulls and four sheet-bronze trumpets found in the dark, still, crepuscular and mordant waters of Lough-na-Shade which Navan overlooks. A severed skull rested in the equally eerie pool at the King's Stables. All about, the hills are dotted with tombs, and at the precise time when the timbers were cut for the great cone, more were cut to construct the palisade at the Dorsey, an even more enigmatic enclosure extending over 120 hectares just south.

Thus, in the elusiveness of facts in a world of Western scholarship obsessed with Greeks and Pharaohs, the North's legends are all that are on offer. Deirdre of the Sorrows first glimpsing her lover Naoise at Conor's court at Emain Macha.

Pushy Queen Maeve, as feckless as any royal ever, envying her husband's fame and baubles, particularly his brown bull, cajoling her armies to steal the white bull of Cooley belonging to the uncouth Conor.

Lough-na-Shade, Navan

Navan in winter

Macha, with her dying breath, cursed Ulster's men to faint
at the sight of a woman's menstrual blood. All save the boy
Cuchulainn, summoned from the Ring of Gullion,
Culainn's land, who rejected the wiles of the bawd
Moreagon and fought on alone at Glendoey, tying himself
upright to a post when wounded, a raven pecking his
wounds to keep him awake. But, this being Ireland, there's
a friend to betray him and Maeve snatches the bull which
later – as the storyteller seeks a moral – gores her to death.

Fearful of everything, of the dark of the forests, of the dark sucking-down of the bog, the timid Mesolithic peoples made fires only by the coast, reached under the kelp for crab, scraped mussel from the rock, cockle from the strand. This new island they had come to had made them prisoners by its shore and thus they made little impression on it.

The Neolithic people were of stouter heart. They understood a fair technology and cleared the forests with their stone axes. They ploughed and sowed and reaped. And made decorated pots. But above all they felt driven to make tombs, great megaliths on the windy hill tops, under which they buried their dead with goods to ease them into the new world. They had a religious fervour and thus they marked this land for ever, as religion has for ever since.

Below and opposite: Slieve Gullion

They marked it with their memorials,
their tombstones, their graves, and their
graveyards.

On each of Gullion's craggy summits
they blessed a grave. On Birra's an eight-
metre lintelled passage leads to an
octagonal burial chamber once corbelled.
Cremation was the dominant burial
practice in these parts at those times.
They left a court-tomb at
Ballymacdermot, a dolmen by a thirty-
metre cairn at Ballykeel, another at
Clonlum, a tomb at Annaghmare. The
Iron Age Celts left us the Dane's Cast
and the Dorsey to puzzle on, the early
Christians, the Kilnasaggart pillar and
Killevy nunnery dedicated to Saint
Darerca, patron of seafarers.

The planters left us Moyry Castle. Lord Mountjoy, Elizabeth's Lord Deputy, had come north to pacify and subdue when the sixteenth century was becoming the seventeenth. He had a Dutch engineer build him the rectangular enclosure and square muskett-looped tower of Moyry to secure the pass into the north before he moved on to create Mountjoy Castle itself on the shores of Lough Neagh.

Next among the forts came Charlemont's, by The Moy, on the banks of the Ulster Blackwater. Another, the East Battery, looked down on Enniskillen from the Fort Hill, its star-shaped outline still detected by the observant. But Charlemont was a different matter, a real heavy artillery star fort with surrounding earthworks and spear-shaped corner bastions. Mountjoy was built to garrison 100 horse and 1,100 foot. The handful of lads at Moyry had the short straw though, right on the edge between terror and ecstasy, and over, in the dark nights.

Those in the sod-ramparted fort thrown up in six days at Mount Norris may have fared even less well. But the towers at Forkhill and Ballintemple held no terrors, mere follies for a landlord class.

Left and opposite: Slieve Gullion

In a world where villages crouch in the sleepy valley, where seas are milky blue and the dipper forages in the plashy stream, the National Trust is chaperone and heir apparent. In the orchard county of Armagh their potpourri governance began centuries after Mountjoy swept out from Charlemont, burning crops, smashing peasants' looms, starving the O'Neills into submission. The manor houses of Ardress, The Argory and Derrymore are theirs for the marketing. Ardress is the house of a gentleman farmer of the seventeenth century, much prettified by local architect George Ensor who married into the Clarke family in 1760. In The Argory, time – as the Trust would want it – stands still, leaving this eclectic house much as Walter McGeough built it in the 1820s.

Derrymore, thatched, and built for the pistol-packing duellist Chancellor of the Exchequer Isaac Corry, who imposed Ireland's window tax, was not immune from the North's recent troubles. The Act of Union had been drawn up in its drawing room.

In the Trust's farm buildings the middle-aged welcome the mummification of their own childhoods. At Benburb, beyond the massive precipitous river-gorge-edge fort another preservation order seeks to bring social balance to each Sunday drive's worthy pedagogy, where each village shall have its history interpreted, sans odour, noise, disease or dirt.

By the banks of the old Ulster Canal, the
Benburb Heritage Centre offers up, spick-
and-span and anodyne, a nineteenth-century
linen mill. And so more Sunday history. In
Ballymoyer is the execrated grave of Florence
MacMoyre, last hereditary keeper of the
Book of Armagh who pawned it for a fiver to
raise the fare to London to inform on the
blessèd Oliver Plunkett, Catholic martyr, for
another mess of potage.

Left: Ballykeel dolmen
Below: The Argory
Opposite: Ardress House

Lough Neagh is the largest freshwater lake in these islands, alder- and reed-fringed, cut off from roads, choppy with frightening squalls in winter, midge-hazed in summer. It is also with its little northern sister, Lough Beg, the North's only Ramsar site, recognised as a wetland of international conservation importance. Finn Mac Cool created it, of course, scooping out its shallow hollow to grab a sod to clod after his departing rival. Missing his target the sod became, we all know, the Isle of Man, where else?

Below: Lough Neagh
Opposite (*top*): Church Island, Lough Beg

Tiny Lough Beg is, with its muddier shore, a haven for waders and surface-feeding birds. Neagh, despite eutrophic pollution, is heaven for other ducks, supporting by far the greatest concentration of diving ducks in this archipelago. Census numbers, though almost unimaginable, are accurate and confirmed winter after winter. Imagine – and who really can? – 100,000 wintering wildfowl: 20,000 pochard, 18,000 tufted duck, 11,000 goldeneye, 4,000 coot, 1,500 scaup swimming in raft-like concentrations, dipping and diving, losing themselves from view as they feed. And the surface-feeders are there too: 4,000 mallard, 1,700 teal, 1,500 widgeon, 80 shoveller.

Crouching in the reed beds, prone in the marshland, anoraked and binoculared twitchers, heavy with flask and sandwich box, check off red-crested pochard, smew, ring-necks and lesser scaup accumulating their daily duck aggregates. Little and ring-billed gull are coffee-break diversions.

Whooper, mute and Bewick's swan lumber into noisesome take-off. Watch them, and marvel, for 6 per cent of the world's whoopers could be there. Lapwing, curlew and golden plover winter in the fields.

Not to have heard the curlew's plangent cry, at misty sun-reddened dusk, nor still-chilled, breath-fogged, grey-lagged dawn, is not to have been tutored in the languages of loss and sorrow. One-eighth of these islands' breeding population of great crested grebe nest on the lough's floating reeds. Shelduck burrow. Mallard and tufted duck build, and this truly is a land of coot and moorhen. Sedge warbler and reed bunting cling to the rushes; a redpoll flashes by.

Autumnalis is a name to conjure with, though *Coregonus autumnalis pollan* may be too much for some. The Lough Neagh pollan, so named by academics, is the fish that time forgot. The last ice age separated it from its nearest co-species the Alaskan cisco and it is well distinct from its English, Scots and Welsh associates: vendace and gwyniad, powan and schelly. Coming up the Shannon after the ice age, it somehow mislaid its normal migratory habits and forgot to go back downstream.

The pollan have now almost disappeared from the Shannon lakes, and the Lower Erne's fish are furtive, old and rare but once, near the mouth of the Six-mile-water, Lough Neagh had a Pollanstown, a cluster of poor riverbank hovels. Spawning in early winter and shoaling in the lough's autumnal afternoon shallows, blue of back, silver of belly, in fact mildly herring-like in appearance, Neagh's five million are Europe's only real pollan. Siberia and the vast Alaskan wilderness have plenty though.

A fresh September pollan, caught sparkling in a seine net from the shore or taken on the fly at dusk, split, boned with a knife sharp enough to skin a fairy, rolled in oat-flake, fried in butter, matched with a floury Ulster spud or two boiled in their skins, is another of the North's most particular and real delights. Not one to be relegated to time's mists, cut off from life, packaged and framed as are the pre-industrial seashore fishermen oh so perjured in the chocolate-box pastels of the province's popular painters.

Forbidden to the Jews, despised by the Romans, gods to the Egyptians, mere delicacies to the ancient Greeks, the common eel is the lough's most prolific fish. They feed here, eating everything they can clamp their jaws on for half a decade, or for a decade and a half, brown- or yellow-bellied, and no one knows of the reasons for their colour choice, no one knows the whys and wherefores of the length of their stay. Then, come some autumn night, wet and moonless, they turn towards the sea, their bellies for the first time silver, their eyes protruding and only their own god, if they have one, knowing why.

Top: Kinnego Marina, Oxford Island
Bottom: Bann Foot
Opposite: Swans at Bann Foot

Out of the lake, up the Bann and west four thousand miles and eighteen months across the Atlantic to the wild Sargasso Sea, a mass of floating weed, to spawn and die. For this is from whence the eels' ancestors came, drifting on the Gulf Stream with the Atlantic Drift, taking three years to do so, metamorphosing as they come, into elvers, less than a hand's breadth long. Some, for some reason, some inexplicable destiny, stay in the Bann's estuary, but most come up river, turning from transparent to black as they do, turning the river black too with their number.

Resting by day, burrowed in the mud, slimy to the touch, en masse, for some they are the stuff of nightmares, for others a source of nudge and ribaldry. By night they feed, nosing at stones as need be to put up a loach or a pollan fry. On warm and stormy nights, heaven forfend, they may make off over the wettened grasses. And who would meet them there being yet of sound mind? And sober? Or who would bathe in the still summer waters when the eel may take to basking too? Such curious matters entrance the imaginative. Alchemists vowed elvers sprang from the hairs of a stallion's tail.

Left: Lough Neagh at Cranfield
Below: Lough Neagh at Antrim
Opposite: Southern shore, Lough Neagh

Out-charmed by the broad and chestnut-shaded squares and Lanyon church of Castlewellan village, and indeed by the regimented elegance of its own farm courtyards, nondescript Castlewellan Castle, austere in its granite bulk, was built for the 4th Earl of Annesley to designs by one William Burn who succeeded in the seemingly difficult, but possibly specifically requested, task of producing a house devised in the fashionable Scots baronial style of the middle of the last century, without a single Scots feature.

It is surely one of the least attractive of the North's
castles. And this despite its lakeside setting. Flanking
the stoic ranks of windows are two towers, one,
oddly, circular, the other not. Inside, in conference,
there are Christian groups. Best then for the traveller
to revel in the courtyards, toy with the sculptures in
the lakeside sculpture trail and ponder on the early
earls – engaging teams to stoke the arboretum's coke
boilers which heated greenhouses better than house.

Castlewellan Castle

South of the Mournes, Newry – where till recently one of the local weekly newspapers was the splendidly titled *Frontier Sentinel* – is William Barre's town, as Belfast is Charles Lanyon's city. Barre, a Newryman himself, ushered in his career by breaking all Unitarian traditions and persuading the elders to choose decorated gothick revival over their tradition of neo-classical; a sense of space belies the church's modest size.

Having given the town his first church (and a bank and his father's tomb), Barre also gave it his last, a curious red and yellow brick potpourri of styles from French flamboyant window, through Lombardesque façade to Rheinish belfry. Banbridge is another Barre town; the snarling polar bears on the town's monument to Captain Crozier, lost on the search for the North-West Passage, is his, as is Seapatrick's church transept. The modest Catholic church at Hilltown is not his.

Top: Castlewellan
Bottom: Mountain road through the Mournes

A road runs through them. Just one real one, they say, prosaically the B27, from Kilkeel's gulls and fish-wet pier north up the valley of the Aughrim river, crawling between Aughrim and Leitrim hill, past Attical, 'tween Slievemageogh and Slievenagore, Pigeon Rock (Eagle Mountain just behind) and Slieve Muck, across Deer's Meadow, Rowan Tree river south, round Spelga Dam to the left, taking the line west between Cock and Butter mountains, wondering all the time if that's the Cock and that's the Hen, why's that the Butter pat. Then north of Hen, along down the valley of the Rocky river, and over the Bann bridge. Into – what town could this be called – but Hilltown?

Here and there the solitary thorn tree stands against the skyline in an open field, its bark grey, its height ten metres, its twigs shiny and red. In spring its white flower clusters have a cloying, wicked smell. The fairy thorn.

Top and bottom:
The Mournes

The Mournes themselves fill up to overflowing the whole south-west portion of the county of Down. Almost 21,000 hectares of granite in as many assorted shades as you could wish, from grey to pink, according to the detail of the granite and the filter of the sometimes menacing cloud, racing behind, dawdling ahead. Add on the purple and madder of the heather, the carmine of the rowan, the mustard of the lichen, the dusty ink of the sloe, the black diamond of the elder and blackberry. Plus albescent fluff of bog cotton, white crystal of snow – enough for any palette. Gorse clumps, prickly, a goat's food, crouch by stone walls, their yellow-oranged flowers vanilla-essenced in a summer's still heat. In the ditches of old loneys pale primroses smile to the open sky. The rowan tree, like the hawthorn a rose by another name, yields scarlet berries. They will speed the hound, prevent bad fire and keep the milk so sweet, and are best eaten, sweetly acid, after frost.

Cut down the fairy thorn and the banshee will get you. And the bourtree, the elder, scalloped by the wind beside the cottage? It's tainted with evil. Give a man a skelp of a bourtree and his hand will follow you out of his grave. Burn the wood in your fire and you'll see the devil in the flames. Fashion an elder-wood cradle for your children and the fairies will change it for a changeling. Still, like people, not all the elder is bad; the berries, squashed, a salve for burns.

The heart of Mourne country

Once the cottages and farms of the Mournes were thatched; but the Welsh slate roof now seems natural, almost feral, in the hills and valleys as do the black, green or red-lead painted corrugated roofs of adjoining barns in the lee of sheltering stands of sycamore. White is the order for the lime-washed walls, though here and there an earth-coloured red suffuses a whole clachan of farms. Bungalows such as the multitudes of those that have transgressed against the edicts of the heritage police across Donegal's hills are few and far between. The metal rainwater goods are lost for ever and the best of ornate iron gates hang hungover from its posts. The barge-boarded Ulster porch with its acutely pitched roof, with echoing twin-matched, roof-attic rooms above, is alive and doing well, as is the also traditional clutch of stapled, over-painted electric wirings running under the eaves as out of a ceramic faucet, but the Georgian sash window – its lamb's tongue profiled wood glazing bars painted white, inner lining frame a thrush's-egg blue - its glass playfully uneven in afternoon sun, is on the list of endangered species. Of villages, bar the appropriately named Hilltown with its Georgian courthouse, there are none, though Mayobridge, deep in country freckled with hill forts, cairns and standing stones, might wish to rub off some glory registering itself in the Mournes' foothills. Rathfriland has a Magennis castle ruin. But not everything is entirely above ground. Drumena cashel contains the most elegant of the North's dry-stone souterrains.

Right: Bloody Bridge
Opposite (*top*): Dundrum Castle
Opposite (*bottom*): Castle Ward

Down by the coast legend and history brush against each other uncomfortably, neither doing the other justice in their tragedies. Maggie's Leap is a chasm, jumped in avoidance of rape, or by a serving girl protecting her virtue from the attentions of a gentleman admirer, if you only wish for the drawing-room thrill. Bloody Bridge, nearby, is so named for Protestants, taken prisoner and massacred in 1641 by the local war lords the Magennises.

Dundrum Castle has its unpleasantnesses too. In its sheer apparent bulk, it was the mightiest of the defensive Norman castles on the Down coast. Greencastle, dating from the same era, south on Carlingford Lough, is impressive enough; Narrow Water, further up the lough, despite its murder hole, seems (though it wasn't) but a decorative folly in comparison. Castle Ward, in this light, is but a frippery.

His back to the Mournes, de Courcy, stragetist, warrior, colonist, scourge of Down and Antrim, had Dundrum erected, on an obviously strategic site, soon after he began the invasion of Ulster in 1177. First he threw up earthen banks, then a massive curtain wall closing off the upper ward. A bridge across a pit guarded the east, a postern the west. Next came the keep, fifteen metres across, with a rock-hollowed cistern basement water supply and one upper floor. The second floor came four centuries later. Entrance was by the first floor, to the south-east, facing bravely into each morning's sun. A spiral staircase leads to the upper storey, once wood-floored, for bedrooms and latrine. The watch patrolled the parapets. Towers were thrown up to improve the gates' defences. King John took the commanding stronghold in 1205, but the Magennises had it in the middle ages. By the seventeenth century the coast was peaceful enough for a house to be built in the lower ward. Centuries before, the Neolithic islanders ranged the sand hills below, leaving just the faintest of traces on the bay: charcoal from a hearth here, post holes from a hut.

Centuries beyond, shelter and defence were secondary, pride reigned. Castle Ward's time had come.

Top: Mourne foothills
Bottom: Sheaves of grain near the Mournes

Jack Sprat could eat no fat, his wife could eat no lean, or, as in the case of the profligate commissioners of Castle Ward, Bernard could not abide the gothick, wife Lady Anne could not stand the classic. So, in 1760 m'Lord Bangor erected Doric columns in his chambers while m'Lady's boudoir ceiling is modelled with huge devices like groups of pendulous angular lactating mammary glands as in Henry VII's chapel in Westminster Abbey. Perhaps her hours in bed were spent admiring the ceiling. There are scandalous persons who said the straight road to Killough was built to hasten Bernard's journeys to his quayside mistress.

William Percy French was a curious cove, a heavily moustached one-time inspector of drains, born in Roscommon, with a facility for composing ever-remembered-afterwards tunes, with comical and catchy words to match. A great man for the soirees, a fine hand at the piano, he enhanced his audiences' amusement and delight by drawing what he called 'smoke pictures' in coloured chalks on brown paper as he sang. At the end of the song he reversed the paper and there, begob, wasn't there another picture entirely, y'er honour? Sued unsuccessfully for libel by the West Clare Railway, he wrote a more plangent composition.

'The Mountains of Mourne', despite its whimsy, its
mocking of Irish institutions, is also an examination
of love's emotions strained by emigration, as emigrant
wish, dream and bravado turn to reality. It also
brought fame to Newcastle, whose birth had been
due to the railway. This is not a verse always sung at
the town's soirees:

> I seen England's King from the top of a 'bus –
> I never knew him, though he means to know us
> And though by the Saxon we once were oppressed,
> Still, I cheered – God forgive me – I cheered wid
> the rest . . .

The Mountains of Mourne at
Newcastle

Opposite (top): Strangford village
Opposite (bottom): Strangford Lough

East of Killough's sycamore-lined and continental boulevard are delightful almshouses, a Lanyon manor in the Georgian manner and St John's Point church, holy well and bullaun stone. North a mile or so is Ardglass, a port synonymous with the bonny shoals of herrin', and the fiefdom of Jordan de Saukeville when King John landed in 1210. It has castles at every turn. The abandoned railway track joining the two ports runs through thick rush beds skirting the cottage-fringed sea, the cottages once home to squatter fisher-families on Lord Bangor's vast demesnes.

Top: Ardglass fishing fleet
Bottom: Ardglass coastline

Inland from Ardglass, in rich drumlin farmland,
Ballynoe stone circles (one, thirty metres across, of fifty
stones some two metres high) stand as at a crossroads of
Neolithic and medieval reference points; a moated rath
and de Courcy's twelfth-century Castle Skrene lie west.
Strangford Lough, named so by the Vikings, is to the
north. Thus, as always on this island, the first human
impressions on the land meld with artefacts imposed
within living memory in the span of a few hectares. In
Ardglass itself the warehouses running down to the
harbour, named as the New Warks, date from 1426 and
encompass Horn Castle. Cowd Castle stands north-
west, Margaret's Castle is but across the road. Jordan's
(for M. de Saukeville) looms above the harbour, across
the square. Isabella's tower is on the Downs.

However, Scrabo Tower, near Newtownards, is but an extravagance, built by Lanyon to decorate the horizon for the Londonderrys of charming Mount Stewart. In the house hangs the definitive Stubbs equine portrait. The family are descendants of Robert, 2nd Marquis, Viscount Castlereagh, draughtsman of the Act of Union, the most hated man in Ireland, who died by his own cutthroat razor and for whom the poet Shelley drafted the epitaph –

I met with Murder on the way.
He had a mask like Castlereagh.

Scrabo Tower and the fertile lands around Strangford Lough

Right: Flax harvest at Seaforde
Below: Flax in bloom at Seaforde
Opposite (*top*): Rape fields and the Mournes

Seaforde of the Fordes is another of the old estates, the original seventeenth-century Castle Navan much burned, much rebuilt. Farming flax and rape, it has a scattering of gatehouses and a stunning maze at whose centre Diana poses.

Clandeboye, near Bangor, is home – for those who love to know – to the Dufferin and Avas. Between the two are many others, not National Trusted 'House, 1–6pm, Apr & Oct: Sat–Sun/Easter; May–Sept: daily (ex-Tues). Private, secluded.

Some are conference centres, schools, hotels; others
are closed but to the cheekily curious. Killyleagh's
Rheinish castle, now marketing its apartments, has
an eclectic history of family disputes and arcane
rents.

Top: Rhododendron petals at
Rowallane, near Saintfield
Bottom: Hillsborough Lake
Opposite: Minnowburn Beeches,
near Belfast

In Hillsborough, a village happily misplaced from an English shire, Colonel Arthur Hill (to whom much thanks) commanded a classic artillery star fort which his more frivolous descendants adapted as a mock-castle. Others added a picnic-party gazebo and an ornamental wooded lake. Beyond, on a steep hill, overlooking all he surveyed, atop a Doric column sprouting from amongst humble bungalows, the 3rd Marquis's statue stands. At the bottom of the hill, up a languid, tree-lined avenue, stands the most elegant church in the North, simplicity in the clean line of planters' gothick; opposite, in bronze, the 4th

Marquis in corduroys, with blackthorn.

Across the square, at the top of this Georgian street
of potpourri sellers, past the antique toll house, the
governor's residence – its governor, his bugler, his
private army gone – awaits another garden party.

And Belfast? The city which held down the world's headlines for twenty-five years in consequence of Ireland's politic having pinned down much of England's for eight hundred years. A city without which no portrait of the North would be complete.

It's a provincial Victorian establishment of pubs, churches, and lost mechanicals. Its commercial focus now a broad ankh, a tall cross with a loop on the top, on a field of red brick, the ankh's top the plaza and plump verdigris-ed dome of the city hall, its cross two boulevards, Donegall Place and Wellington Place–Chichester Street, a pack of shuffled British chain stores, banks and insurance offices.

Yes, it has all the makings of a real city, a city of red buses, black taxis, a baroque opera house, a few late Victorian bars, three newspapers, two radio stations, two television stations, a distinctive accent, new cinemas, parking meters,

football teams, a dog track, empty night-time streets and an ice rink. Its challenging northern wit, its Presbyterian Sunday ethos rubbing surprisingly easy shoulders with its welcoming wee-cup-of-tea-in-yer-hand hospitality.

Beyond come diminishing rows of red brick terraces, distressed warehouses, chirpy city villages, rich leafy suburbs, an encircling ring of hypermarkets and DIY stores. Then the green drumlins, a coast being swallowed by golf clubs, market towns, some scarred by tribal war, others more in danger from rash cheap design, the lingering odours and detritus of their fast-food outlets, their pubs where the only afternoon sound is the rubric of the four-letter word, the only evening sound the boom of country and western. And yet it's magic.